OCT 10 2017

D0486523

100

THINGS TO DO IN
NAPA VALLEY
BEFORE YOU
DIE

St. Helena Library
1492 Library Lane
St. Helena, CA 94574
(707) 963-5244

A Gift From
ST. HELENA PUBLIC LIBRARY
FRIENDS&FOUNDATION

• •

MARCUS MARQUEZ

REEDY PRESS

Copyright © 2017 by Reedy Press, LLC
Reedy Press
PO Box 5131
St. Louis, MO 63139, USA
www.reedypress.com

No part of this publication may be reproduced or transmitted in any form or by any means, electronic or mechanical, including photocopy, recording, or any information storage and retrieval system, without permission in writing from the publisher.

Permissions may be sought directly from Reedy Press at the above mailing address or via our website at www.reedypress.com.

Library of Congress Control Number: 2017934537

ISBN: 9781681060989

Design by Jill Halpin

Cover Image Credit: Bob McClenahan
Interior Images Credit: Kevin Medici

Printed in the United States of America
17 18 19 20 21   5 4 3 2 1

Please note that websites, phone numbers, addresses, and company names are subject to change or cancellation. We did our best to relay the most accurate information available, but due to circumstances beyond our control, please do not hold us liable for misinformation. When exploring new destinations, please do your homework before you go.

DEDICATION

For my wife, who has been a partner to all my ventures and adventures. For my two boys, who make living in Napa Valley even more amazing than it already is.

• •

CONTENTS

• •

• •

● ●

● ●

• •

· ·

ACKNOWLEDGMENTS

I would like to acknowledge and thank my parents and family, who helped me experience some of the great things Napa Valley has to offer. Without their endless invitations to go to dinner and hang out at wineries when I was a lot younger, I would have never been exposed to a lifestyle of passion and entertainment that I now am blessed to live every day. Without your influence and your view on life, I would not have been able to appreciate the bounty that we are surrounded by.

I would like to thank Sunshine Market, Bistro Jeanty, and Don Giovanni's for being part of what made me fall in love with Napa Valley. Visiting the region early on with my wife created some of my favorite memories. My wife, Kolea, and I would spend many afternoons trying new places for our own research and ended up falling in love with the area. Without her input throughout these many years, I would not have been able to put this "100" list together.

I have to thank Victoria Zurakowski, a fashion blogger who helped me stay focused and organized and ensured that I made it to the finish line. To my faithful assistant, Eliana Gallegos, I have to give huge thanks because without her I would not be able to juggle all the fun projects that get thrown at me. Mark S. Allen, thank you again for always having a way to make people feel special and for making this project happen. Without Mark S. Allen my 100 things to do would have been a list kept to myself. To Andy and Trisha

Florsheim for believing in me to partner with them to build a place of their dreams in St. Helena. To Stacia Dowdell for giving me the opportunity and letting me join you with creative foresight on co-creating a Napa Valley destination. All of these people had major influence, and I am grateful for their help getting me to where I am and contributing to this book.

A big thank you to all the people in Napa Valley who contribute their heart, sweat, and soul so all of us get to go out and enjoy this special part of the world. A special thanks to everyone I work with at the winery and restaurants! All of you make me a better person and strive to be a part of something bigger.

FOREWORD

When I was first approached to write *100 Things to Do in Napa Valley Before You Die,* I panicked. Mentally, the number "100" seems to be a lot, and in some respects it is. For example, living until you're a hundred years old would be really impressive, and scoring a hundred points in a basketball game would also be quite a feat.

After the initial shock wore off, I quickly came to my senses. I soon realized that I could write about a great many things, since Napa Valley is simply bursting at its borders with wineries, restaurants, boutiques, cafés, bars, tasting rooms, galleries, outdoor activities…the list goes on and on. But you're about to read about some of the best things to see and do in this region.

This whole writing experience has helped me understand that there are many more than 100 things to do in Napa Valley before you die—the area has more than 500 wineries alone to visit! Please follow me on instagram @originalmarmar, and visit my website, www.100thingsNapaValley.com, to see more of what Napa Valley has to offer.

Every single day here is a new adventure, a new beginning, and I can't wait to share it with you. My advice to any person who's visiting Napa Valley is to embrace the laid-back way of Wine

Country life and immerse yourself in the new experiences that you'll surely find while you're here. Dare to be a little different, and take everything that's thrown at you. Don't be afraid to go off the beaten path because that is where many of our hidden gems lie. Don't worry if you can't do everything you want/plan to do (very few do) because I can guarantee that you'll be planning your next visit before you even finish this one.

As soon as you enter the Wine Country, you'll get that Napa Valley feeling—a feeling that will stay with you for a lifetime. So, what are you waiting for? It's time to start checking off all these awesome Napa Valley experiences from your bucket list.

Enjoy your stay in the Wine Country, and if you're ever looking for me, you'll find me anywhere the music meets the vines!

Marcus Marquez
Your Personal Concierge
IG: @originalmarmar #100thingsNapaValley

INTRODUCTION

Welcome to Napa Valley—the epitome of scenic countryside vistas, legendary wines, expansive estates, quintessential charming towns, chic luxury lodgings, and a highly acclaimed and explosive food scene. Yes, this is the Napa Valley!

Inspirational and awe inspiring, Napa has given many a writer solace in the rawness and drunkenness of this area; as the esteemed Scottish poet and novelist Robert Louis Stevenson once said, "Wine is poetry in a bottle."

Stevenson, who penned his candid travel memoirs *Silverado Squatters* while honeymooning in Napa Valley, also discovered the pleasure that the Valley could evoke. "Find out where joy resides, and give it a voice far beyond singing. For to miss joy is to miss all . . ." (*Silverado Squatters*, 1883) and joy he found among the craggy rock faces and rolling countryside.

Approximately a one-hour drive from San Francisco, her famous neighbor, Napa Valley is California's not-so-secret gem and, probably more importantly, its most famous wine region. Home to well over 500 wineries, its nickname "the Wine Country" is no accident. It's a wine and food connoisseur's heaven, and we invite you to come and explore the region's signature full-bodied Cabernet Sauvignon, buttery Chardonnay, and much more!

• •

Wine lovers and foodies from neighboring San Francisco and the rest of the Bay Area flock religiously to the Valley for a natural getaway. It's also the perfect vacation spot for any person who wishes to pair serene landscapes reminiscent of Provence and Tuscany with sensational wines, captivating cave and winery tours, and some of the best Michelin-starred restaurants in North America . . . romantics be warned!

Despite its luxury destination status and rampant celebrity following, the area has no pretense, and formality is virtually absent. This is one place in California where smart jeans are perfectly acceptable in many of the finest restaurants.

While harvest time is a popular time to visit Napa Valley, every season creates its own magic. Springtime brings new growth and beauty as the emergent grape leaves transform the Valley's hillsides into a carpet of brilliant lush green dotted with bands of contrasting mustard blossoms. As the Valley begins to warm up and summer nears, a plethora of events and festivals beckons, creating what can only be described as a buzz. Fall is a hive of activity and brings the "Crush," as vineyards, wineries, and workers bustle tirelessly to gather grapes for their next vintages. When winter finally settles in and brings a crisp calm, insiders know this is the time to snap up coveted reservations in the Valley's world-famous restaurants and bars, hit downtown for a spot of holiday shopping, enjoy the festive spirit in the prettily decorated towns, and take some much needed time out in some of the most exclusive spas and resorts. Napa Valley is a place you'll never tire of, since there's always something to do or something going on, no matter the season.

Napa Valley is a transformative utopia made up of a number of small towns, each of which is unique. In the southern part of the Valley lies American Canyon, a family-friendly, affordable base with a great many fun activities. A mere fifteen-minute drive up north, you'll find Napa, a chic and trendy area, with a thriving food and drink scene. Yountville is located right in the heart of the Valley, and this is where you'll come across scores of luxury boutique hotels, resorts, and restaurants, including the three-star Michelin-rated The French Laundry. Head to Oakville and Rutherford, where the eminent Robert Mondavi Winery presides and Cabernet rules the region. St. Helena, located up the Valley, is a magical place. Its Main Street is lined with stylish boutiques, fashionable jewelry stores, quirky cafés, and unique art galleries. For rest and relaxation, visit the spas and resorts of Calistoga, where you'll be able to immerse yourself in restorative mud baths and calming mineral pools for a blissful day of pampering.

Expect the unexpected, and enjoy every moment of your time in Napa Valley. This is truly a place where you'll be able to pursue your favorite activities and explore new, untapped interests. Be prepared to fall in love because nothing can quite prepare you for the splendor that awaits you here in the Wine Country.

CULTURE AND HISTORY

WINES, CHEESES, AND PROVOCATIVE ART
AT PEJU PROVINCE WINERY

Located in Rutherford, this family-owned estate has welcomed guests for a number of years to sample its stunning array of wines while immersing themselves in a faraway world of art and culture. Experience some Wine Country hospitality at its finest as you navigate the winery's beautifully manicured grounds, which showcase a fine collection of sculpture and installations. Peju is dedicated to producing balanced, expressive, and elegant wines from its certified organic and sustainably farmed vineyards. Specializing in Cabernet Sauvignon, this wine country oasis is home to world-class hospitality and culinary experiences.

The winery art program is led by Christopher Hill Gallery, which dedicates itself to the works of local esteemed artists together with new emerging artists from around the world. See art through new eyes and be taken on an emotional journey.

8466 St. Helena Hwy., Rutherford
800-446-7358
www.peju.com

TIP

Experience Peju's small-farm cheese and wine pairings or its "farm to table" wine and culinary explorations for a true epicurean journey.

WATCH A WORLD-FAMOUS SHAKESPEARE PERFORMANCE
AMONG THE VINES AT NAPASHAKES

NapaShakes . . . it could translate as many things, but theater lovers and Shakespeare fans know it for what it is—a memorable theater experience that celebrates the life and times of one of history's greatest playwrights—the one and only William Shakespeare.

Travel back in time and discover how Shakespeare was really performed. The venue, described as a mini-Globe Theater, allows audiences to experience Shakespearean theater at its finest. Watch some of your favorite Shakespeare plays come to life on stage among the vines and tendrils of Napa Valley's idyllic landscape—we're sure Shakespeare would've approved!

1299 Pine St., Suite A, St. Helena
707-963-3115
www.napashakes.org

UNDERSTAND A TRUE VISION
OF ART AND WINE AT HESS WINERY

The Hess Winery has put itself on the international map for wine, food, and art. Founded more than twenty-five years ago, it has earned itself a solid reputation in the wine and culinary world.

Other than its impressive wines, Hess Winery is home to the Hess Collection—it's very own contemporary art museum.

The Hess Collection's head chef also brings a lot to the table (in more ways than one). Made with locally sourced organic products, individual tapas-style dishes are uniquely paired to complement both the wine and art.

4411 Redwood Rd., Napa
707-255-1144
www.hesscollection.com

CABERNET IS LIFE!

Silver Oak has so much wine history and one of the best Cabernet Sauvignons in Napa Valley. Its unique style, which uses American oak, balances the flavor of the fruit and the cooperage that millions love. "Life is a Cabernet" is what they live by. Enjoy a tour and tasting, and take your picture next to the iconic white water tower. Take home the current vintage, and share it with your friends. Silver Oak was founded in 1972 and has grown into a state-of-the-art winery. It has a glass house library with vintages dating back to the '70s. You will find one of the best tasting room teams in Napa Valley, and their friendliness and expertise is sure to be a highlight of your trip. Their wines will leave you wanting more! Luckily for you, you can find Silver Oak in most of your favorite restaurants and steakhouses across America!

915 Oakville Cross Rd., Oakville
707-942-7022
www.silveroak.com

TIP

Do not miss the best release party in Napa Valley. Buy your tickets early, and plan your Napa Valley vacation around it. Silver Oak's Napa Valley Cabernet Sauvignon release is always the first Saturday of February, and its Alexander Valley release party is always the first Saturday in August. See you there! Make sure you tag them with #LifeisaCabernet.

TREAT YOUR EYES
AT MA(I)SONRY

Part tasting room, part art gallery, part furniture showroom, part store . . . this is one trendy spot to take in some serious art and culture with a difference. If you're looking to be inspired by aesthetics, look no further because Ma(i)sonry (pronounced MEY-SUH-N-REE) is the place to go.

Ma(i)sonry boasts an impressive wine portfolio together with a tasteful collection of artwork and furniture, which adds to the exclusivity, making it more reminiscent of a private club than anything else. The beautiful home furnishings date back to the early sixteenth century and have been skillfully paired with contemporary works. It's a designer's paradise! Don't forget to bring your wallet. Every item is for sale!

6711 Washington St., Yountville
707-944-0889
www.maisonry.com

TIP
To load up before having a few drinks, check out Tacos Garcia for a cheap street food option. You'll find them outside Pancha's dive bar across the street.

DIVE INTO THE ONLY DANCE PARTY
IN ST. HELENA!

Anna's Cantina. You have probably heard about this place in St. Helena but couldn't find it. At night is when this place turns itself on. Anna's Cantina claims to be the best bar in St. Helena—not because it is the only bar in town but because of the friendly staff, great décor, and mix of clientele, creating the perfect atmosphere for your night out. I have to say that some of the best Napa Valley nights end there. You will find yourself drinking with some of the legends of the valley or be drowned out in a wedding party crowd. Nonetheless, you will have a great time! Make sure you call to see what is going on before you stop in. It can range from watching sports to karaoke to a DJ and a dance party. Or just relax and enjoy a game of pool and Anna's great jukebox. Some people say that what happens at Anna's stays at Anna's.

1205 Main St., St. Helena
707-963-4921

TIP
Bring cash so that you don't have to go back in the morning to retrieve your forgotten credit card.

TAKE IN SOME LOCAL HISTORY
AND HAVE SOME FAMILY FUN
AT NAPA VALLEY MUSEUM

Head along the St. Helena Highway to Napa Valley Museum for a perfect day out with the family and a great break from wine tasting (if you need a break!). You'll be able to learn all about the region through the museum's permanent collection, which showcases art and other treasures.

The city limits sign proves the humble beginnings of the Valley, with an initial population of a mere thirteen people. Take a tour of winemaking through the years through a series of paintings and photographs and pay homage to those wine pioneers responsible for putting the region on the map and producing those gorgeous wines you've been sipping.

55 Presidents Cir., Yountville
707-944-0500, www.napavalleymuseum.org

TIP
If you want more in-depth information through the eyes of a local expert, plan your museum trip for the third Saturday of every month, which is when you'll be able to join a guided tour.

CELEBRATE SUMMER
AT THE NAPA COUNTY FAIR

Napa Valley in any season is exciting, but if you're there for the summer, be sure to catch the Napa County Fair. It's a summer sizzler that celebrates everything Napa's about—food, wine, art, history, and culture.

Watch live chef demonstrations while soaking up the atmosphere with live music and watching people laugh, dance, and have a good time on the streets. The wine pavilion is a must to sample some new wines, and you'll also be able to participate in unique olive oil tastings.

Street entertainers, collaborative art projects, fireworks, and even bull riding can all be found at the Napa County Fair.

1435 N Oak St., Calistoga
707-942-5111
www.napacountyfair.org

TIP
Be sure to catch the 4th of July celebration and parade. This is a 4th of July celebration with a difference. Where else are you able to participate in a reds, whites, and blues wine tasting?

TAKE A PEEK
INTO CALIFORNIA'S RURAL HERITAGE

When you think of California, one of the last words that's likely to pop into your mind is "rural," but the state is not all glitz and glamor on the red carpet. It also has a rich rural heritage.

Bale Grist Mill State Historic Park is worth visiting for many reasons. You'll be able to take a peek into the rural heritage of the Valley, and the park's restored water-powered gristmill is impressive (it still grinds grain today).

The slow-turning old grindstones give fresh meal the perfect consistency for making a range of scrumptious breads that are synonymous with old times, including cornbread, shortening bread, yellow bread, and spoon bread.

3369 St. Helena Hwy., St. Helena
707-963-2236
www.napaoutdoors.org/parks/bale-grist-mill-state-historic-park

TIP

Add a hike to your history-filled day, and enjoy the moderate 2.4-mile History Trail that will eventually connect you to Bothe-Napa Valley State Park. Look out for historic points of interest along the way, such as the White Church and Pioneer Cemetery.

RIDE THE VALLEY'S WINE TRAIN
IN STYLE

One of the most popular forms of travel to go cross-country in California is by train, so it's no surprise that Napa Valley has its own train dedicated to wine, food, and travel. This experience will definitely help you live a life people write novels about. You can't go to the Wine Country without doing it!

Experience charming, ethereal scenery and some of the best wines on a fully functional antique train. Polished brass accents and intricately etched glass partitions add to the train's authenticity. Dining in the train's gourmet wagon restaurant is all part of the experience, and if you're a foodie, you'll most certainly enjoy the ever-changing seasonal menu.

1275 McKinstry St., Napa
707-253-2111
www.winetrain.com

TIP

Feel like eloping? A gorgeous vintage setting together with upscale gourmet dining sets the scene for the perfect elopement. As the train moves along the rails, take in the lush, sweeping scenery around you and exchange vows with the one you love in an intimate ceremony.

JOIN A PHOTOGRAPHY EXCURSION
WITH THE "ART OF SEEING" TOUR

Would you like to improve your photography skills? Do you feel that the "art of seeing" has abandoned you?

With two local experienced photographers, you'll go on a mesmerizing journey into the depths of the Valley as you learn how to interpret the world around you and capture it through your lens.

Customized tours are available. If have a vision in mind, call the studio to discuss your options so you can take different images of what you want while freezing moments to reveal the true beauty of Napa Valley. We guarantee that your Instagram feed will soon be awash with compliments and likes.

1225 Division St., Napa
707-480-4003
www.artclarity.com

PLAY WINEMAKER FOR A DAY
AT JOSEPH PHELPS VINEYARDS

If you've ever daydreamed of opening your own winery, you can begin learning the tricks of the trade by playing winemaker for a day at iconic Joseph Phelps Vineyards. In this unique experience, you'll learn the art of blending their flagship wine, Insignia, which consists of six signature components. After stomping your grapes (OK, you don't actually do that!), you can compare your blend with the current Insignia vintage. This is one of the fastest ways to become a winemaker. Go straight to the top, and show off your very own bottle of wine to your friends. Time to work on your branding!

200 Taplin Rd., St. Helena
800-707-5789
www.josephphelps.com

TIP
Gaze out from the terrace onto the winery's private ranch, where rows upon rows of vines can be seen.

LOSE YOURSELF
IN A WORLD OF WINE AND ARCHITECTURE AT CADE WINERY

You will often find an intimate relationship between beautiful wines and world-class architecture. One of my favorite architectural features is the rock wall at Dominus Winery. Unfortunately, it is not open to the public, but you can taste its attention to detail in every bottle of wine it produces. I urge you to visit the website! For those bent on seeing unique wine country architecture in person, Cade Winery, designed by Juancarlos Fernandez, is a sustainably designed, Gold LEED (Leadership in Energy and Environmental Design)-certified winery estate. Looking out from Howell Mountain, you can enjoy a glass of the winery's crisp Sauvignon Blanc, which pairs perfectly with stunning views of the valley below, but be sure to snag a bottle of its estate Cabernet Sauvignon, since you'll want to continue the experience when you get home!

360 Howell Mountain Rd., Angwin
707-965-2746
www.cadewinery.com

TIP

The work of Signum Architecture partner Juancarlos Fernandez can be found across Napa Valley. My personal favorites are Brand Winery, Brasswood Estate & Winery, Hall Winery, and Sinegal Estate. And the wines at these places are as beautiful as the architecture.

GO ON A CULINARY ADVENTURE
AT THE CULINARY INSTITUTE OF AMERICA

If you have ever wanted to be a professional chef, here is where you can learn the tricks of the trade. Delve into the world of food, and take your culinary skills to a whole new level. You have many courses to choose from, including Entertaining for the Holidays, Cooking at Home, Artisan Breads, and Tasting Wine Like a Pro, but we're pretty sure you'll be able to master that last subject after just a few days in Napa Valley. Dine at their student-run restaurant, and stay current with their calendar to see what they have to offer. If you can't make the trek up to St. Helena, the CIA at Copia in Napa is equally inspiring, hinging food concepts on the fertile Napa Valley and the institute's on-site gardens.

2555 Main St., St. Helena
707-967-1100
www.ciachef.edu/cia-california

TIP

If you crave the latest in culinary devices, be sure to swing by the CIA lifestyle retail store, which offers everything from linens to gadgets that even top chefs will admire.

EXPERIENCE THE WONDER
THAT IS OLD FAITHFUL GEYSER

California's Old Faithful geyser earned its name by erupting on a regular basis, and it's also known as a pretty good earthquake predictor! Whatever its practical talents, the geyser's natural beauty will leave you breathless.

Old Faithful's grounds are home to a well-known goat farm, which is perfect for a family day out. You'll even get to meet the famous Tennessee Fainting Goats.

You'll also get the chance to stroll around the picturesque, tranquil gardens, which offer spectacular panoramic views across Robert Louis Stevenson State Park and the Palisades.

1299 Tubbs Ln., Calistoga
707-942-6463
www.oldfaithfulgeyser.com

TIP

The Old Faithful Geyser is one of the most photographed natural spots in California, so make sure you have your camera ready to capture the many rainbows forming in its misty sprays.

SPORTS AND RECREATION

WITNESS SPECTACULAR VISTAS
AT WESTWOOD HILLS PARK

Westwood Hills Park is many things. It's home to the Carolyn Parr Nature Museum, and it's the perfect getaway for those looking for new and exciting hiking trails that cut through stunning groves and verdant meadows. If you love nature but you're not a seasoned hiker, Westwood Hills is ideal.

Here, lush vegetation is ubiquitous. The park is home to many varieties of trees, but the eucalyptus is widespread, as you'll discover once you reach the canyon.

Pack a picnic basket, and take a little break on the way in a grassy meadow or at one of many picnic tables in the area.

3107 Browns Valley Rd., Napa
707-257-9529
www.napahiking.com

UNWIND AFTER A DAY OF WINE TASTING
AND RELAX AT MEADOWOOD SPA

There are many reasons to stay at Meadowood, but perhaps the best is gaining access to one of the most elevated spa experiences in the Valley. Besides the three-star Michelin restaurant, croquet, golf, and lovely rooms, the spa treatments, which are open only to members and hotel guests, are amazing. Because of the spa's regular celebrity clientele, privacy and personalized comfort are at the top of the list at Meadowood. Sessions begin with an in-depth conversation with a spa therapist, and strategically designed suites, which include a private bathroom, steam shower, and tranquil views off a built-in seating area, allow guests to maintain privacy between any number of delicious treatments. Begin with the ninety-minute Essential Journey, or go all in with the three-and-a-half hour vinotherapy experience, From the Vines—but whatever you choose, you really can't go wrong. The spa also offers experiences specially designed for men.

900 Meadowood Ln., St. Helena
707-531-4799
www.meadowood.com/spa

VISIT THE WORLD'S BEST GOLF COURSES
IN THE HEART OF THE VALLEY

Golf enthusiasts will be in golf heaven in the Wine Country. You can choose from a wide variety of scenic golf courses throughout the region, including Silverado Golf Club. Situated right in the heart of Napa Valley, this VIP golf course is only for members and resort guests. Featuring a great many water crossings, various elevation changes, and oak woodland, this challenging yet picturesque golf course sets the standard. It was redesigned by PGA Hall of Famer Johnny Miller and is home to the Safeway Open PGA Tour. You can come out and watch pros do what they do. You can choose from great packages once you book your stay, including Sunday Funday, Couples Escape, and Golfers Dream. Judging from the names alone, you know you will have a great golf experience.

Silverado Golf Club
1600 Atlas Peak Rd., Napa
707-257-0200
www.silveradoresort.com/golf

Vintner Golf Club
7901 Solano Ave., Yountville
707-944-1992
www.vintnersgolfclub.com

TIP

If you are not staying at the Silverado Resort, you can play nine at the Yountville Vintners Golf Club, which is a public golf course. You are still in Napa Valley playing golf, and you might find me and my family there on Sundays!

STAY ON A HOUSEBOAT, WATER-SKI, AND CHILL
AT PLEASURE COVE MARINA

Wine isn't the only liquid that deserves credit in Napa Valley. There's also Lake Berryessa—a lake so great in so many respects—measuring a staggering twenty-three miles long and three miles wide!

The lengthy lakefront offers up numerous gems, but if you're looking for something a little different, head to Pleasure Cove Marina, which can be found on Lake Berryessa's southwestern shore. A serene spot, this beautiful area is the perfect place to become one with nature. Rolling grass hills, giant oaks, and a wide variety of wildlife, including deer and wild birds, are just a few things you'll get to experience at Pleasure Cove Marina.

128 Hwy. #6100, Napa
707-966-9600
www.goberryessa.com

TIP
Are you looking for some accommodations with a difference? What about a houseboat? Rent a fully equipped deluxe houseboat—they come in different sizes and can accommodate up to twelve guests.

ATTEND A STAR PARTY
IN THE DEPTHS OF THE WINE COUNTRY

Look up at the sky and get lost in its beauty. Vast open spaces and clear unpolluted skies coupled with temperate weather make for the perfect stargazing session.

It doesn't even matter whether or not you're interested in star names and constellations. The Napa sky is always pretty impressive at night.

Imagine being in the middle of nowhere and the only sound you can hear is your own breath as you observe stars, star clusters, and galaxies. It's the perfect opportunity for a little bit of storytelling.

Always look for a new experience to enjoy wine. This will be a night you can never do again. Be in the moment. The best viewing dates are near the new Moons.

707-569-6800
www.winecountrystarparty.com

STAY FIT,
BE CALIFORNIAN,
AND WORK OUT IN NAPA VALLEY

California has always been associated with health and wellness. Join fitness classes, enjoy customized fitness programs, participate in a boot camp (if you dare), or work on your body conditioning and mind in one of the area's many yoga studios. For fitness, you're in the right place. As well as being a wine lover's refuge, Napa Valley is also a prime fitness destination.

If you're just passing through, you won't want to sign up for a membership, but many of the Valley's state-of-the-art fitness centers offer temporary memberships, walk-ins, and concession cards. While working out in Napa, you can also indulge in even more wine and food.

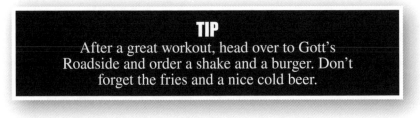

TIP
After a great workout, head over to Gott's
Roadside and order a shake and a burger. Don't
forget the fries and a nice cold beer.

Napa Valley Total Fitness
835 Lincoln Ave., Napa
707-320-2301
www.napavalleytotalfitness.com

Pure Barre Napa
Bel Air Plaza, 3632 Bel Air Plaza, Napa
707-257-7215
www.purebarre.com

Core Values Health & Fitness
1660 Silverado Trail, Napa
707-888-1910
www.corevalueshf.com

Health Spa Napa Valley
1030 Main St., St. Helena
707-967-8800
www.napavalleyspa.com

In-Shape
120 W. American Canyon Rd., American Canyon
707-644-4110
www.inshape.com

RIDE THE TIDE
AND PADDLE THE NAPA RIVER

For something a little different, rent a board, and then paddle and navigate your way down the river from one of three paddleboarding rental spots along the way.

This sociable and recreational activity is perfect for the entire family and includes a full induction session onshore so that you can fully enjoy your experience.

If you're not confident about taking to the waters alone or you want to experience as much of the river as possible, join a stand-up paddleboarding tour with experienced paddleboarders and learn about everything you see along your way.

730 Water St., Napa
707-666-1628
www.napavalleypaddle.com

TIP
Stand-up paddleboarding is an awesome workout, and you're likely to work up an appetite. Add the picnic-by-the-river option to your tour, and enjoy some delicious local food and Andrew Lane Napa Cabernet.

GO KAYAKING
ON THE NAPA RIVER

Life jacket, check. Paddle, check. Kayak, check. Bucket loads of enthusiasm, check. You're ready to go! Channel that adventurous person within, and have a fun-filled day on the Napa River.

Rent a single kayak—or a double, if you're game—and navigate the beautiful Napa River. The river's perfect for all levels, from beginners to the more gung-ho advanced kayakers.

An activity for the whole family or the individual traveler, traveler, kayaking comes with your own sturdy paddle and kayak so that you can head down the river at your own pace.

100 Riverside Dr., Napa
707-277-7364
www.enjoy-napa-valley.com

TIP
Want more out of your kayaking experience? Join an exciting and wet kayaking tour to discover some of the river's most hidden pockets.

HIKE
NAPA'S EASTERN RIDGELINE

Prepare to enter a whole new world. With more than fifteen miles of hiking trails, all of which are dog friendly and diverse in appearance, you'll be able to enjoy a walk at your own pace through some of Napa's most rugged landscape while enjoying the natural serenity that Lake Hennessey has to offer.

Whether you're an avid hiker or just an ambler through nature, a trail is available for everyone. If you're lucky, you might even spot some of the park's intriguing wildlife, such as mountain lions, deer, bobcats, black bears, gray foxes, and coyotes. For those curious about birds, white egrets, woodpeckers, great blue herons, loons, hawks, golden eagles, and even bald eagles have all been spotted in this area.

2602 Chiles Pope Valley Rd., St. Helena
707-259-5933
www.napaoutdoors.org/parks/moore-creek-park

TIP
Are you an equestrian or a mountain biker? A great many abandoned dirt tracks await you.

PUT ON YOUR HELMET,
REV THE ENGINE, AND EXPLORE NAPA BY HARLEY

Keep calm and Harley on . . .

Are you a Harley lover? Has it always been your dream to ride one? Whatever your reason, there's probably no more exciting way to explore the Wine Country than zooming through it on what would have to be the sexiest bike in the world, which is why having the opportunity to rent a Harley-Davidson for a day or two can't be missed. They say coming back to return the bike is what's hard.

Be prepared to fulfill that childhood dream!

1132 Main St., St. Helena
707-758-3919
www.niemansmotorcyclerentals.com

TIP
Take a peek al the metal art on display at the shop, and admire the Cold War–era bomber plane engine out front!

GO ON A HOT AIR BALLOON ADVENTURE
ALOFT THE VALLEY

Up, up, and away . . . float up, soar across the skies, and check out Napa Valley from a bird's-eye view.

Get away first thing in the morning, and catch a glimpse of California's not-so-secret gem from above. If the timing is right, you'll even be able to witness Napa's sunrise, which is spectacular.

Glide two thousand feet above the Valley, and enjoy a delicious gourmet continental breakfast or brunch while on board.

Get carried away and create memories that last!

Napa Valley Aloft
6525 Washington St., Yountville
855-944-4408, www.nvaloft.com

Balloon Above the Valley
603 California Blvd., Napa
707-253-2222, www.balloonrides.com

Napa Valley Balloon, Inc.
4086 Byway E., Napa
707-944-0228, www.napavalleyballoons.com

Calistoga Balloons
1458 Lincoln Ave. #15, Calistoga
707-942-5758, www.calistogaballoons.com

GO BIRD WATCHING
IN THE AMERICAN CANYON WETLANDS

The Wine Country has some of the most extensive water systems and wetlands in the country. In fact, you might be interested to know that the American Canyon Wetlands form the largest estuary on the Pacific Coast in either North or South America.

This unique hiking trail offers two contrasting landscapes. To the east, you'll see a typical suburban neighborhood, and to the west, huge open spaces and a large body of water. Nature lovers will feel at home, and you're bound to spot a variety of local birds along the way are popular, as are American avocets. Enjoy yourself in the rawness of the open spaces, and see how many you can name.

2 Eucalyptus Dr., American Canyon
www.cityofamericancanyon.org

TIP
Relax after your hike by soothing your muscles at Spa Gaia and enjoying a complete Asian spa treatment experience.

GET YOUR CREATIVE JUICES FLOWING
WITH SOME NAPA ART CLASSES

We were all created to create, and there's no better place to do it than in one of the most inspirational and scenic places on earth. When you eventually return home and try to explain your travels and experiences in the Wine Country, words might fail you. Sometimes what you'll see and experience will be almost indescribable, which is when your art will speak.

If you're looking to nurture your artistic side, Nimbus Arts can offer expert help. Course tutors will help you foster creative expression, pulling it from deep within you even if you don't think you have it. They offer a range of classes for all ages and skills, from glass blowing to pottery to painting.

649 Main St., St. Helena
707-963-5278
www.nimbusarts.org

GET DOWN AND DIRTY
IN NAPA'S MUD BATHS

Napa's high volcanic ash content hasn't just created the ideal terroir for viticulture. It's also helped create something even more unusual to the area—revitalizing mud baths.

The idea of mixing ashy soil with hot mineral water to form natural hot springs was first introduced by native Indians. It didn't take long for the sensation to take off, and it soon became the must-do thing in terms of your health, wellness, and beauty.

Immerse yourself in the waters of one of the many natural hot springs in the area. Indulge in a long mineral soak, and treat yourself to a treatment or two, including luxury massages, aromatic body wraps, and therapeutic mud masks.

Calistoga Spa Hot Springs
1006 Washington St., Calistoga
707-942-6269, www.calistogaspa.com

Dr. Wilkinson's Mudbath Resort
1507 Lincoln Ave., Calistoga
707-942-4102, www.drwilkinson.com

Indian Springs
1712 Lincoln Ave., Calistoga
707-942-4913, www.indianspringscalistoga.com

Solage Calistoga
755 Silverado Trail N., Calistoga
707-266-7534, www.solage.aubergeresorts.com

TOUR THE VALLEY
BY BICYCLE

Nothing can compare with the simple pleasure of hopping on a bike and riding, and it's also a fantastic way to explore the region. If you have your own bike, great, cycle your heart out, but if you don't, countless bike rental outlets are available where you can rent a bike for a day or for however long you need it.

Unless you're familiar with the area, you should consider exploring the Valley's terrain with a seasoned tour guide, who'll not only be able to take you to the must-see places but also to those that only the locals know about . . . shhh, don't tell anyone!

St. Helena Cyclery
1156 Main St., St. Helena, 707-963-7736

Calistoga Bike Shop
1318 Lincoln Ave., Calistoga, 707-942-9687

Napa Valley Bike Tours and Rentals
6500 Washington St., Yountville, 707-251-8687

Napa River Velo
680 Main St., Napa, 707-258-8729

Backroads Bike Tours
Napa Valley Bike Tours and Rentals
6500 Washington St., Yountville, 707-251-8687

TIP

The Tour de Cure is a fund-raising bike ride in which you can raise cash for the American Diabetes Association. It is usually run during the first weekend of May. You can register online for ten, twenty-five, fifty, eighty, or if you're really game (or crazy enough) one hundred miles. After finishing, expect even more wine tasting, dancing, eating, and enjoying massages!

GET INSTAGRAM HAPPY
AT NAPA VALLEY'S MOST PHOTOGRAPHIC SPOTS

We might be biased, but ask anyone else and they'll agree—Napa Valley is truly a spectacularly photogenic place. Those obsessed with Instagram will love tagging their pictures with #wishyouwerehere and #Ilovenapavalley. To pick one over another is hard, but you must take a picture in front of the Napa Valley sign! Follow it up with the Grape Crusher Statue just to make sure they believe you were here! #100thingsNapaValley Tag me at @originalmarmar when you do!

The Grape Crusher Statue

Welcome to Wine Country. This sign is one of the first that tells you you've arrived at your destination. You can find it toward the south of Napa on Vista Point Drive.

The Napa Valley Sign: Welcome to this world-famous wine growing region

Here's your bragging right. Prove to your friends you're in town and make them jealous. Choose one of two signs to pose by, both of which can found on Hwy. 29. You will want to remember the famous saying "the wine is bottled poetry."

PLAY BOCCE WITH THE PROFESSIONALS
OF ST. HELENA

Pick up the *St. Helena Star* and, after reading the hilarious police log, move to the sports page and find the weekly standings of the famous bocce league in St. Helena. If it is the right time of year (seventeen weeks played in the spring and summer), you can pick any night and watch some of the best bocce playing you will ever see. Drink wine and mingle with the locals. It is the best opportunity to see how Wine Country folks relax. If you get a chance to roll a few, that is a bonus. If you want to play as a guest, the bocce league has six pages of rules and regulations, so you will have to pick up a game outside of bocce league hours. This league has been here for more than thirty years, and with more than fifteen hundred players on 122 teams, it is one of the largest bocce leagues in Northern California.

Crane Park, Bocce Courts
360 Crane Ave., St., Helena
www.cityofsthelena.org

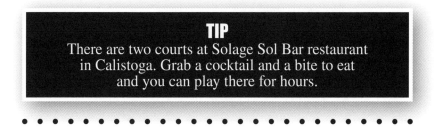

TIP
There are two courts at Solage Sol Bar restaurant in Calistoga. Grab a cocktail and a bite to eat and you can play there for hours.

FOLLOW IN THE FOOTSTEPS
OF ROBERT LOUIS STEVENSON

Want to see where Scottish novelist and poet Robert Louis Stevenson was inspired to write *Treasure Island*? Aptly named after the writer, Robert Louis Stevenson State Park covers an impressive 5,272 acres and offers some of the most awe-inspiring views in the region from its highest peak, Mount Saint Helena.

This is also where Stevenson took his new bride for their honeymoon, which was in an empty bunkhouse of the Silverado Mine. Some would say he was a true romantic—but others might disagree.

Be a little daring and hike up to the summit of Mount Saint Helena. The Robert Louis Stevenson Memorial Trail offers you a little history along the way, and a marble statue now marks the spot of the old bunkhouse.

Lake County Hwy., Calistoga
707-942-4575
www.napaoutdoors.org/parks/robert-louis-stevenson-state-park

TIP

Hike Mount Saint Helena on a clear day and be treated to some bonus views of the Pacific Ocean, Mount Shasta, Mount Lassen, and the Sierra Nevada mountains in the distance.
How many peaks can you name?

MUSIC AND ENTERTAINMENT

GET THE VIP TREATMENT
AT THE BOTTLEROCK FESTIVAL IN NAPA

Forget Coachella and other well-known music festivals around the world. If you want to experience a few days of eclectic bliss, music, and gourmet food, the BottleRock Festival seems an obvious choice.

Presented by JaM Cellars, this three-day festival in May that celebrates diversity, freedom, and style takes place in the heart of Napa at the Napa Valley Expo. JaM Cellars also has a tasting room in Downtown Napa that you have to check out.

The festival has established itself as one of the coolest to get tickets to. Watch some of the world's most famous bands and artists perform in an unpretentious, relaxed atmosphere, soak up the sun, sample some fabulous new craft ales, and party nonstop.

573 3rd St., Napa
707-253-4900
www.bottlerocknapavalley.com

JaM Cellars
1st St., Napa
707-265-7577

TIP
Have the ultimate festival experience with the special three-day VIP pass, which offers even more exciting perks, such as unlimited access to the VIP Village, live acoustic performances, international DJ sets, and VIP-only bathrooms.

BRING IN SPRING NAPA VALLEY STYLE
AT THE YOUNTVILLE LIVE FESTIVAL

Bring in the spring Wine Country style at Yountville Live. An annual event every March, this is the ultimate experience in luxury exclusive festivals, featuring some of the hottest recording artists from around the world.

Festivalgoers and foodies alike will relish every single moment as they lie about on the grass and listen to some cool beats and sample exquisite foods and award-winning wines. This is a true epicurean experience with the sophistication that is Napa Valley. You'll love every moment of this internationally acclaimed event that's like no other.

www.yountvillelive.com

TIP
Flocks of eager festivalgoers gravitate to the area during Yountville Live, so be sure to book your restaurant choices ahead of time to avoid any disappointment.

WATCH A MUSIC PERFORMANCE OF A LIFETIME
AT UPTOWN THEATRE

Uptown Theatre features some of the world's biggest names, such as Chris Isaak, Boz Scaggs, Beck, Wynonna Judd, Dana Carvey, Pat Benatar, Ziggy Marley, Lyle Lovett, and Citizen Cope, so it's fair to say that it is the number one destination for live performances (of any kind).

Even before you sit back and enjoy a performance, take in the atmosphere and architecture that make this theater unique. Located in Napa's famous West End district, this historic Art Deco landmark that dates back to 1937 is worth visiting just for its history.

1350 3rd St., Napa
707-259-0123
www.uptowntheatrenapa.com

WALK THROUGH THE CONTOURS AND VINES
AT ROBERT MONDAVI WINERY

The Robert Mondavi Winery has a long history thanks to its namesake and winemaking pioneer.

The architecture alone will leave you in awe. A true California-style structure that gracefully sprawls across a vast courtyard with striking arches and statues, it is both impressive and welcoming.

Step inside the bright, open tasting rooms, where you'll be able to sample some rare and special release reserve wines. Art also has an important place here, so be sure to explore the grounds at your leisure and enjoy a range of art, installations, sculpture, and more.

7801 St. Helena Hwy., Oakville
707-226-1395
www.robertmondaviwinery.com

VISIT YAO MING FAMILY WINES
TO EXPERIENCE CELEBRITIES, WINE, AND FUN

A tall order for winemaking? We think not! If you're a basketball fan, you've probably heard of the legendary NBA star Yao Ming. Not just a celebrated sportsman, Yao Ming is also known for his humanitarian work and more recently his winemaking at his Napa Valley estate—Yao Family Wines.

Sourcing some of the highest-quality grapes in the region, Yao Family Wines has managed to create some award-winning, full-bodied fruity wines, including its signature wine, the Yao Ming Napa Valley Cabernet Sauvignon.

Exclusive tastings, wild rock 'n' roll performances, gourmet bites, basketball- and wine-themed events—all we can say is "Fun!"

920 Main St., St. Helena
707-968-5874
www.yaofamilywines.com

DISCOVER THE MAGIC IN CRAFT BEER
AT MAD FRITZ BREWING

"Compelling" and "understated" are great words to describe one of the region's hottest craft beer breweries. Mad Fritz Brewing produces high-quality, barrel-aged beers that have won over beer fans throughout the state, and the waiting list for club membership is impressive. Minimalistic in its style and premises, you'll find Mad Fritz Brewing tucked among some of the big-name wineries and tasting rooms just off St. Helena's main street.

Beer lovers will appreciate the range of classic beer styles with a twist. Pale lagers, blue corn pale ale, and rye stout are among the many beers produced. We predict great things for this brewery that performs beer magic.

La Fata St., St. Helena
707-968-5058
www.madfritz.com

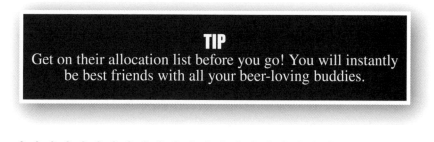

TIP
Get on their allocation list before you go! You will instantly be best friends with all your beer-loving buddies.

TASTE WINE IN LUXURY
AT STAGLIN FAMILY VINEYARD

The epitome of a true family-run vineyard, the Staglin owners pride themselves on their custom. With a long history that dates back to the Civil War, this is one winery that has been successful in combining tradition with modern practice.

The land is farmed organically, and the owners see themselves very much as stewards. Sustainability is just as important. The winery uses solar fields to produce all the power at the modern underground production facility.

To witness an authentic passion for wine, visit the winery for an intimate tour of the well-kept estate and underground production caves, and sample the impressive portfolio of Cabernet Sauvignon— it's happiness in a glass!

1570 Bella Oaks Ln., Rutherford
707-963-3994
www.staglinfamily.com

EXPLORE A PRIME WINE SPOT
AT TRINCHERO FAMILY ESTATE

The Trinchero wine journey began when a young Italian immigrant in search of a new life headed west and purchased a derelict Prohibition-era winery. Its story is as captivating as its wines.

Art aficionados will appreciate the precision and detail of this winery, located just north of St. Helena, as well as the high-caliber wines. A luxury wine label, Trinchero sources grapes from its single vineyard and a few prime appellations to craft exceptional blends.

Visit this extensive estate, and take a leisurely stroll through its beautiful grounds, but don't forget to make the most of true Wine Country hospitality with the winery's Single Vineyard tasting.

3070 St. Helena Hwy., St. Helena
707-963-1160
www.tfewines.com

TIP
There is so much to see here. Join Trinchero's Legacy Club to keep in touch with everything that is happening. They have wines that you will enjoy on all occasions.

SEE WHERE EAST MEETS WEST
AT NEWTON VINEYARDS

For more than thirty-five years, Newton Vineyards has been producing some of the best-quality wine in the entire state. More than five hundred acres of steep slopes covered in vines with picture-perfect panoramic views are just part of what makes this Chardonnay-producing vineyard special.

With its unique architectural design, the winery blends seamlessly with its natural surroundings, but it's the extras that set it apart. Well-manicured, English-inspired rose gardens with a Chinese pagoda and lanterns all add to the idiosyncrasy.

Travel through time and experience the winery's awe-inspiring barrel cave and gardens followed by a professional yet relaxed seated tasting that showcases a range of award-winning wines from the portfolio.

2555 Madrona Ave., St. Helena
707-204-7423
www.newtonvineyard.com

TIP

If you visit Newton Estate, be sure to ask for its signature Cabernet Sauvignon, which has been aptly named The Puzzle. Every year the makeup of this showpiece wine remains a mystery.

LEARN ABOUT WINEMAKING
DURING THE 1800s AT SHAFER VINEYARD

To say that Shafer Vineyard has been in the winemaking business for years is an understatement. Dating back to the 1880s, this thirty-two-thousand-case winery that sits prettily between rugged mountains today produces five stellar wines that exemplify the region.

While the winery is known for its portfolio of all-star reds, it's the signature Hillside Select Cabernet Sauvignon that exudes the unique fullness and grace of fruit that exemplifies the Stags Leap District.

When you visit this family-run winery, you'll be welcomed warmly and introduced to a flight of sumptuous wines in an informal seated tasting that brings together new and old friends.

6154 Silverado Trail, Napa
707-944-2877
www.shafervineyards.com

TIP

Ask about Eighty Four. It is a fun and exciting new project from Doug Shafer and winemaker Elias Fernandez.

BE CHARMED BY INK HOUSE INN
WITH THE ULTIMATE LUXURY EXPERIENCE

If you want a peaceful, undisturbed stay while in the Wine Country, The Ink House makes for a charming Northern California break. Everything from the classic wooden exterior exterior to its sense of history to the idyllic views of rolling countryside and well-manicured gardens exudes sentiment and splendor. A promise of beauty, The Ink House won't let you down. It's indulgence at its finest.

If you enjoy anything classic, you'll appreciate the authentic antique accents and furnishings that add to the private rooms' luxury. You'll also be taken in by the heavenly lawns that encompass the home as well as the pretty gardens and vast orchards. It's here that you'll be able to meander, picnic, and enjoy something else California is famous for—the sun!

1575 St. Helena Hwy., St. Helena
707-968-9686
www.inkhousenapavalley.com/inn

TIP

For "open access" to the chef's impressive kitchen, aperitifs and digestifs, private tours of the Spring Mountain Estate, and private educational wine tastings, book the ultimate Ink House Experience.

TAKE IN UNPARALLELED PRIVACY AND PEACE
AT POETRY INN

Perhaps the name's no accident. Poetry Inn, which sits on a hill in the coveted Stags Leap District, evokes deep emotions and stimulates the mind. Many a guest has said that if it weren't for dusk falling, they could remain on the inn's ridge all night, observing and taking in the magic of the Valley. Overlooking wine paradise, there's simply no denying that it's privy to some of the best vistas in the entire state.

When in the Wine Country, one must indulge. Your luxury guestroom is both spacious and filled with the finer things—from plush bathrobes to wood-burning fireplaces, this is where romance can come to life. A three-course gourmet breakfast with all the trimmings is also the perfect way to begin a day of wine tasting.

6380 Silverado Trail, Napa
707-944-0650
www.poetryinn.com

TIP

For world-class dining, you'll be able to take your pick from a number of renowned Napa Valley restaurants, including Bouchon and The French Laundry, which are just a short drive down the hill.

HAVE A ROMANTIC STAY
AT AUBERGE DU SOLEIL

Nestled among Napa Valley's celebrated vineyards is an exclusive chic boutique hotel amidst an olive grove not too dissimilar to Napa Valley's French sister, Provence. You'll soon understand why Auberge du Soleil has been dubbed one of the country's most romantic hotels.

Each *maison* is private, with its own terrace. Custom furnishings, wood-burning fireplaces, the hotel's hillside location, and almighty views of vineyards below add to the charm and romance.

In true Mediterranean-inspired style, the renowned Michelin-starred restaurant features a colorful menu using the freshest seasonal ingredients. As well as a top-rated restaurant, the hotel also boasts a world-famous luxury spa and an impressive fifteen-thousand-bottle cellar.

180 Rutherford Hill Rd., Rutherford
800-348-5406
www.aubergedusoleil.aubergeresorts.com

TIP

Auberge du Soleil has its own sculpture garden, which is worth a separate visit itself. The "park" features around 110 sculptures from sixty-five California-based artists. While you're there, do not miss the sunset and view from the terrace. It is truly one of my favorite spots.

GET SERIOUS ABOUT YOUR WINES
AT 750 WINES

Calling all serious wine enthusiasts. Whether you're a taster, drinker, or collector, a trip to St. Helena's 750 Wines, the region's finest wine store, is a must!

Enjoy a personalized and private tasting in a spacious yet minimalistic setting, where you'll be able to sample some of those hard-to-come-by wines that are considered "off the beaten path." Concrete walls are lined with wines you just wouldn't see elsewhere; Robert Foley, Lail, Araujo, and Grace Family are just a few of the names that decorate the shelves at 750 Wines.

At 750 Wines, it's all about the personal touch. Tell David, the owner, your preferences, and enjoy tasting those limited edition wines you have always dreamed about.

1224 Adams St., Suite C, St. Helena
707-963-0750
www.750wines.com

HEAD TO A
LOCAL FAVORITE
AT STONY HILL VINEYARD

A favorite winery among the locals, Stony Hill Estate offers a special experience, which makes the winery's isolated location seem not so far away. With a long history, it's also the oldest family-run winery in the Spring Mountain District that's still in operation today.

Brace yourself to travel back in time. A trip to Stony Hill Vineyard will conjure up images of what it was once like in Napa when the area was still relatively untouched and undeveloped. It's not as crowded as some other more populated parts of the Valley, and the region has a distinct agricultural feel to it.

Indulge in an intimate and casual gourmet wine tasting while admiring the vistas looking to the east of the Valley toward Howell Mountain. We're pretty sure you'll fall in love with the winery's authenticity and rustic ways. It's worth a visit!

3331 St. Helena Hwy. N., St. Helena
707-963-2636
www.stonyhillvineyard.com

APPRECIATE UNIQUE WINE TASTINGS
AT WHITEHALL LANE WINERY

Since 1970 the Leonardini family and Whitehall Lane Winery have been producing some of the finest wines in the Valley. Despite the winery's contemporary front and design, the property is still home to some of the original farm structures, including an old storage barn that predates 1900.

The winery owns 140 acres of prime land covered in vineyards. Its signature Cabernet Sauvignon is a winner in everyone's books, and the Chardonnay and Sauvignon Blanc are both crisp and refreshing.

Wander the boutique winery while taking in the architectural wonder. Art enthusiasts will be especially interested in the vast array of contemporary art on display. With many tasting experiences offered, it's hard to know what to pick, but I recommend the barrel tasting, the food and wine pairing, and the wine and chocolate pairing. It's hard to pick just one!

1563 St. Helena Hwy., St. Helena
707-963-9454
www.whitehalllane.com

VISIT A TRUE "DESTINATION" WINERY
AT DARIOUSH WINERY

There's a reason the owner, Iranian-born Darioush Khaledi, states that visiting Darioush Winery "is both a destination and a journey." This is one visually intriguing winery, which specializes in producing some of the best premium wines in the Valley.

With so many special experiences allowing guests to discover new foods and wines while immersed in a curious world of culture and heritage, you won't be disappointed, especially if you manage to catch one of the estate's many special events, such as dining under the stars.

4240 Silverado Trail, Napa
707-257-2345
www.darioush.com

TIP
Pair your library vintage with the Cowgirl Creamery's artisan cheese range and you'll most certainly engage all your senses and awaken your taste buds.

BECOME ENCHANTED
AT PULIDO~WALKER WINERY

This exclusive visit is invitation only, so the man to know is Pulido~Walker's Estate Ambassador, who also happens to be the president and founder of DMH Napa Valley, a premier destination management agency that specializes in making the impossible possible. Just email Daniel Ha at Daniel@dmhnapavalley.com. Pulido~Walker is an extension of a dedicated wine-loving couple's passion for everything wine related, and their Mount Veeder Estate and winery are testaments of this passion.

Their pursuit of the possible has resulted in an impressive collection of fine wines, which is 100 percent aligned with their philosophy. Spanning more than fourteen thousand square feet, this is a true luxury wine-tasting destination. You'll relish the ambiance as you sample what can only be described as exquisite wine.

1477 Partrick Rd., Napa
707-226-1900
www.pulidowalker.com

TIP

Once you connect with Daniel, you will be guided to the next level of wine experience and a wine availability that is normally saved for celebrities and wine aficionados.

HAVE A REGAL WINE-TASTING EXPERIENCE
AT B CELLARS

You'll find this beautiful and modern winery on the historic Oakville Cross Road nestled in a hillside among rugged, rolling country. As soon as you step onto the estate, you'll notice a blend of comfort and agrarian, character that sets the scene for the unique and intimate wine-tasting experience to follow.

Travel down into the depths of the estate's caves, explore the impressive barrel storage, and sip what can only be described as some of the finest wines ever blended. While exploring the estate's caverns, you'll come across the Grand Salon, a banquet-cum-events room like no other, and as you finally emerge from below, you'll be greeted by magnificent views of the Vaca Mountain range. It's a heavenly vision and well worth the visit!

703 Oakville Cross Rd., Oakville
707-709-8787
www.bcellars.com

TIP

If you thought B Cellar's food was divine, check out their website so that you can re-create that blissful culinary-wine pairing in the comfort of your own home. If you've got a favorite recipe that pairs well with B Cellar's wine, share it and you may be published!

TASTE YOUR WAY
AROUND YOUNTVILLE STARTING AT BOUCHON

Yountville is a foodie's dream come true, and "Restaurant Row" on the town's main street is something quite extraordinary. One of my all-time favorites is a Michelin-starred restaurant serving real French bistro fare in elegant old-world surroundings. Bouchon, created by Thomas Keller, has been a longtime stomping ground for my wife and me since it opened in 1998. Sitting at the bar with a bottle of champagne and ordering the fresh harvested oysters and the *pommes frites* . . . well, it just does not get much better than that. You can then move on to pretty much anything else on the menu once you finish that first course. The fragrant *moules au safran* are simply divine!

6534 Washington St., Yountville
707-944-8037
www.thomaskeller.com

TAP INTO THE EXPERTS' KNOWLEDGE
AT THE NAPA VALLEY WINE ACADEMY

Anyone who has ever worked in the wine industry is familiar with WSET (Wine and Spirit Education Trust). Anyone who is serious about learning how to properly taste and discuss wine has also heard about it.

The Napa Valley Wine Academy welcomes wine aficionados to take on a challenge and embrace some thorough wine and spirits education with a difference.

The Napa Valley Wine Academy is WSET approved and offers a range of courses depending on your level, knowledge, and skill. From sommelier courses to one-day spirit workshops, this is the perfect institute for any wine or spirit buff.

2501 Oak St., Napa
855-513-9738
www.napavalleywineacademy.com

BOUNTY HUNTER
DOWNTOWN NAPA

In 1994, Mark Steven Pope cashed in his 401(k) and drove from New York to Napa in his Chevy pickup truck in hot pursuit of his vision. He started Bounty Hunter Rare Wine & Spirits as a one-man operation with a telephone, fax machine, and notepad. Today, twenty-three years later, his wine and spirits catalog has an annual circulation in the millions. Bounty Hunter's elite clientele has enviable access to the greatest wines that Napa Valley—and the world beyond—has to offer. Special small-lot selections of Cabernet Sauvignon, red and white Burgundy, single malt Scotch, and fine Kentucky straight bourbon have made this an unbeatable source for "great stuff" unlike anything else in the Valley. With a focus on matchless customer service and the rarest of the rare, it's no mystery why the Bounty Hunter and his perpetually packed Wine Bar and Smokin' BBQ restaurant have become Napa Valley institutions.

975 1st St., Napa
707-226-3976

STOP OFF AT PRESS
AND SAVOR ITS BLENDS

You'll love PRESS in St. Helena for a number of reasons. Renowned for its delectable dishes, this atmospheric restaurant is of a dignified caliber. The wine list is accompanied with a knowledgeable wine team that can answer any of your questions and guide you into a new wine world that you did not know existed. There is a serious wine book written by one of their sommeliers available for collectors that you can purchase while you are there.

PRESS features a variety of scrumptious award-winning dishes that showcase local seasonal produce and high-quality meat cuts. Meat lovers will especially relish the smoke-roasted lamb and poultry that are slowly grilled to perfection on a custom-built wood-fired grill. PRESS also has two working gardens from which it sources its fresh organic fruit and vegetables to ensure that its guests are treated to nothing but the best.

587 St. Helena Hwy., St. Helena
707-967-0550
www.pressnapavalley.com

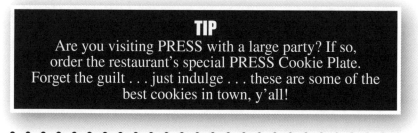

TIP
Are you visiting PRESS with a large party? If so, order the restaurant's special PRESS Cookie Plate. Forget the guilt . . . just indulge . . . these are some of the best cookies in town, y'all!

SIT BACK AND RELAX
IN A RUSTIC SETTING
AT FARMSTEAD

This is farm-to-table food at its finest. Experience this open-kitchen space on a ninety-acre working vineyard and indulge in some serious farmhouse cooking. Farmstead's homegrown wines together with its grass-fed lamb and beef and fresh organic produce make for enjoyable rustic dining.

Locally sourced sole served with wood-roasted cauliflower is a lunchtime favorite, as is the buttery sautéed potato gnocchi that comes with braised greens and a celery root puree. Locals love this place, and everyone has their own favorite. Enjoy the party atmosphere and the great people-watching!

738 Main St., St. Helena
707-963-4555
www.longmeadowranch.com

TIP
The most relaxing coffee break is at Farmstead's outdoor cafe. Enjoy Stumptown coffee and doze off while lounging on comfortable Adirondack chairs. This is what living in Napa Valley is all about.

SEE HOW TECHNOLOGY AND TRADITION INTERTWINE
AT PALMAZ VINEYARDS

Nothing is ever going to prepare you for Palmaz Vineyards' impressive one-hundred-thousand-square-foot subterranean wine cellar, located in Coombsville.

The fermentation dome is arguably the best part. Its claim to fame is that it's the world's biggest underground reinforced structure. The height of the cave alone is equal to that of an eighteen-floor building!

Producing a Burgundy-like Chardonnay, a number of flavorsome Cabernet Sauvignons, and a wine that is rare for the region (Riesling), Palmaz will allow you to discover and savor some delicious, full-bodied wines.

4029 Hagen Rd., Napa
707-226-5587
www.palmazvineyards.com

SAY "PROVECHO"
AND EAT MEXICAN IN NAPA VALLEY

Mexican food is a favorite around the world. It's like an explosion of taste and color all in one, and thanks to the prominent Mexican community, Napa Valley is rife with a selection of great Mexican restaurants. Sometimes you just need a decent burrito! One of my all-time favorites is C CASA in the Oxbow. Nothing says heaven more than a "taco lounge." Enjoy a tasty taco with spicy ground lamb or buffalo in a bustling food court. All food is made to order from seasonal ingredients and sustainable fish and meats. This is a great stop for those watching their gluten intake. You will probably visit it one more time before you leave. C CASA has also received a Michelin Bib Gourmand, which is impressive since you order at a counter.

610 & 644 1st St., Napa
707-226-7700
www.myccasa.com

TIP
Be sure to stop by Villa Carona, Azteca,
and La Luna in Rutherford.

READ VINTAGE BOOKS AND TASTE EXCLUSIVE WINES
IN CHATEAU MONTELENA'S LIBRARY

If you're a wine lover who seeks excellence in everything from the initial tasting experience to the last drop, visiting this historic Napa winery is a must!

Producing age-worthy classic wines, Chateau Montelena Winery, which is cleverly carved into a hillside overlooking a well-manicured Chinese garden, has been attracting avid wine drinkers and collectors for some time.

Join a unique semi-private tour that offers a wine-tasting experience like no other, and learn all about the founder's vision thirty-five years ago and how he brought his dreams of producing a first-growth standard of estate Cabernet to fruition.

1429 Tubbs Ln., Calistoga
707-942-5105
www.montelena.com

ENJOY A LUXURY STAY
AT MEADOWOOD

Tucked away and slightly hidden within the realm of Napa Valley, you'll find a private luxury resort known for its classy establishments and sports venues. Golf, croquet, hiking, tennis, and swimming . . . take your pick and enjoy.

Be prepared to embark on numerous unique experiences. Prestigious wine-tasting journeys, five-star rejuvenating luxury spa treatments, immaculate playing surfaces for golfing enthusiasts, and well-manicured lawns—this is luxury at its finest. The resort is also home to one of the best restaurants in the Valley, and with its three Michelin stars, it continues to impress with its traditional food.

900 Meadowood Ln., St. Helena
707-531-4788
www.meadowood.com

MICHELIN STAR
AT BAR TERRA

This UpValley Michelin-star-rated restaurant offers a fusion of Californian-cum-Japanese-inspired dishes. Housed in a nineteenth century farmhouse known as the Hatchery, this should be on your list to try. The restaurant is one experience that will take you back in time to a classic white-tablecloth restaurant. This is a lost art. Fortunately, if you can't get a reservation to the restaurant, you can enjoy the same techniques from the chef in the bar. I love this place. The ramen is one of the best you will ever eat. How many times can you say you have had ramen made by a Michelin-starred chef? Terra is loved by the locals, and you always leave happy. The attention to detail in the quality of ingredients shows as you pair the food with some of the special wines from the area. This is making me hungry and wanting to go there now!

1345 Railroad Ave., St. Helena
707-963-8931
www.terrarestaurant.com

TIP
Take your time and order everything.
It is a culinary party in your mouth.

TAKE IT ALL IN
AT CASTELLO DI AMOROSA WINERY

There's something about Castello di Amorosa that makes it the idyllic setting for a winery. This thirteenth-century–inspired Tuscan castle is truly impressive. Be sure to take all the pictures that you can. The views are amazing.

Hidden away in the Western Hills of Calistoga, this impressive estate spans 171 acres. It's easy to become swept up in the magic that is Castello di Amorosa, and if you're anything like us, you'll allow yourself to get lost in the land of make-believe.

Castello features a whopping 107 rooms in total, 90 of which are solely dedicated to winemaking and the storage of wine. When you visit their website, you will see some of the incredible parties you can attend, from their Hot Havana Nights to the NYE party. Become a wine club member to receive a special price.

4045 St. Helena Hwy., Calistoga
707-967-6272
www.castellodiamorosa.com

MEET THE ANIMALS
AT CONNOLLY RANCH IN NAPA

Enter a world of farming, ecology, and sustainability, and prepare to be both entertained and educated at the same time.

From fun organic farming and gardening to learning all about how nature can sustain us, you'll leave the ranch happy and more knowledgeable about the world around you.

A number of farm animals here are always a hit with the children, especially during the springtime when new babies join the community.

3141 Browns Valley Rd., Napa
707-224-1894
www.connollyranch.org

TIP
If you want to enjoy a kid-free day out, check out the ranch's website and see what's offered. You might just be lucky enough to catch a one-day excursion solely for kids. Imagine that!

GET LOST IN WINE HISTORY
AT CHARLES KRUG WINERY

Napa Valley trivia: Charles Krug had the first tasting room in California. The winery, the oldest in Napa Valley, has been around for 156 years and has been family owned for seventy-five. At Charles Krug, you can enjoy the estate tasting while having charcuterie curated from the winery's cafe, Cucina di Rosa (named after matriarch Rosa Mondavi). What makes this tasting so special is that you get to try wines exclusive to their estate that are not available in stores. Outside is one of the most stunning parklike properties in Napa Valley. Grab your picnic provisions from the Cucina, and head out and relax under the two-hundred-plus-year-old oak trees. The best thing about this property is that you could actually get married here or hold a luxury wine country event. Every time I am there I always want to bring my friends and celebrate. When you walk in the winery, you are seeing history all over the walls. The redwood walls are from the old tanks bought by Peter Mondavi Sr. and his family and were repurposed throughout the winery.

2800 Main St., St. Helena
707-967-2229
www.charleskrug.com

TIP

A little inside fact on the Mondavi family: granddaughter Angelina Mondavi is the only female winemaker from the Mondavi family. Look for all her exclusive projects at www.amondaviconsulting.com (the consulting winemaker for Brasswood Cellars!).

ESTABLISHED 1876 BERINGER . . .
NEED I SAY MORE?

The great thing about Beringer is that its Chief Winemaker is Mark Beringer, great-great-grandson of Beringer Vineyards' founding brother Jacob Beringer. Even though he is new to the winemaking at Beringer, his family has quite the history of making wine in Napa Valley. With all types of tastings available on this massive estate, one that stands out is the Private Reserve Vertical tasting. You are tasting the finest, most exclusive wines that Beringer has to offer. You are greeted by a personal host and escorted to a private tasting salon in the historic Rhine House. Then you will begin to taste a library of vintage Beringer flagship Private Reserve Cabernet Sauvignon. Once you are done, head over to the gift shop and pick out something for that special someone. Join the club, or check out the event page on the website. There is sure to be something you would want to attend. Beringer checks off all Napa Valley wish lists, from music to picnic events. Let me know about your favorite Beringer experience! #100ThingsNapaValley

2000 Main St., St. Helena
707-302-7530
www.beringer.com

INDULGE IN A WINE AND CHEESE HAVEN
AT V. SATTUI WINERY

Imagine a winery that produces more than sixty kinds of wines! To many this might seem unfathomable, especially for maintaining high quality, but V. Sattui Winery does it with ease!

Established in 1885, this family-owned sprawling property nestled beneath an ancient Valley oak forest has a long history of creating top-rated vintages. Cheese lovers will be in heaven, too, with its impressive on-site cheese shop that sells more than two hundred varieties of cheese. You can take all the great food you purchase at the shop and have a picnic at one of the many tables spread out across the lawn. This place is also great for large groups.

111 White Ln., St. Helena
707-963-7774
www.vsattui.com

TIP
If you can, head to V. Sattui during the weekend for its weekly weekend BBQ, where you'll be able to sample fresh deli-sourced organic foods right off the grill.

IMMERSE YOURSELF IN SPLENDOR
AT SCHRAMSBERG VINEYARD

Schramsberg Vineyard has many claims to fame. It's a favorite among some of the best sommeliers in the world, not to mention U.S. presidents (it's been served by eight successive ones), and it's a popular choice for many a high-end diner in and around Northern California.

The friendly team will greet you with welcoming arms and take you on a tour of a lifetime around the well-manicured grounds. As you wander, you'll also get to sip on some extraordinary sparkling wines. Who needs a celebration for bubbles? The exquisite cave tour, which is a fusion of gothic and romance, and the wine tasting by candlelight will remain ingrained in your memory forever! Try to attend Camp Schramberg, which is known as one of the best adult camps in the country. Book early because it fills up fast.

Schramsberg Vineyard
1400 Schramsberg Rd., Calistoga
707-942-4558
www.schramsberg.com

Davies Vineyards
1210 Grayson Ave., St. Helena

TIP

The Davies family (the family that owns Schramsberg) just opened a new tasting room in St. Helena. You can try their red wine program featuring many famous vineyards in Napa Valley.

HAVE AN INTIMATE EXPERIENCE
AT SILO'S

A stone's throw away from the Napa River Inn lobby, you'll find the historic Napa Mill, which is where the legendary Silo's bar is located.

If you're looking for an exciting musical experience, this place will exceed all expectations. Hailed as one of the Valley's most intimate venues, Silo's seats approximately fifty couples, meaning that when you go you'll have the perfect view because everyone's at the front!

Silo's attracts a host of regional bands and independent musicians, all of whom love performing there thanks to the venue's warmth and hospitality.

530 Main St., Napa
707-251-5833
www.silosnapa.com

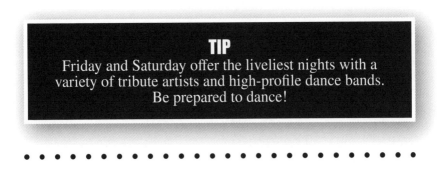

TIP
Friday and Saturday offer the liveliest nights with a variety of tribute artists and high-profile dance bands. Be prepared to dance!

HAVE AN APPELLATION EXPERIENCE
AT HALL RUTHERFORD WINES

On a clear day, the panoramic picturesque views that overlook Napa Valley far below will most definitely capture both your imagination and your attention.

Only a few Napa Valley wineries can truly say that they have more than one physical location, but Hall, located toward the end of a secluded road, is one!

The tour is something else. Highlights include walking through a fourteen-thousand-square-foot cave constructed from handmade Austrian bricks that date back centuries. Art enthusiasts will love the inclusion of modern art displayed among the cave's alcoves. The grand finale of the tour ends in the winery's spectacular tasting room that boasts a brilliant Swarovski crystal chandelier, where you'll be treated to four appellation-specific reds.

56 Auberge Rd., Rutherford
707-967-2626
www.hallwines.com

GET SOME POSH CHOPS
AT MUSTARDS GRILL

Eating your greens has never been as much fun as it is at this iconic roadhouse that serves up a range of tasty Californian-American dishes. If you're looking for simple gourmet American-inspired cuisine, Mustards Grill is one of the hottest dining hubs in Yountville.

Cut into a juicy Mongolian pork chop, a half-pound Niman Ranch hamburger, or if you're game, some aromatic BBQ baby back ribs. Enjoy your meat feast teamed with some freshly dressed green salad that's been grown on-site. The wine list is just as impressive, featuring a number of delicious wines from California and the Northwest.

Mustards Grill is a place where you will find the locals dining and celebrating life! Get there early if you don't have a reservation, and find a spot at the bar.

7399 St. Helena Hwy., Yountville
707-944-2424
www.mustardsgrill.com

TIP
Be sure to check out the restaurant's adjacent organic gardens and farmland, which are responsible for providing the restaurant with around 20 percent of its fresh produce.

FIND OUT WHAT CHANEL AND WINE HAVE IN COMMON
AT ST. SUPÉRY ESTATE VINEYARDS

St. Supéry Estate Vineyards is a one hundred percent sustainably farmed winery in the renowned wine-growing region of Rutherford. You'd expect this winery to be ultra-stylish since it's owned by Chanel, one of the world's leading luxury fashion brands, and it doesn't disappoint!

Committed to creating the best of the best when it comes to handcrafted estate wines, St. Supéry is known for its crisp Sauvignon Blanc and smooth Cabernet Sauvignon. The gourmet melt-in-your-mouth cheeses and charcuterie will impress just as much as the estate's range of delicious award-winning wines.

8440 St. Helena Hwy., Rutherford
707-963-4507
www.stsupery.com

FILL UP ON WINE
AT DEL DOTTO

Take a ninety-minute tour around Del Dotto's hand-dug historic caves, which date back to 1885, and you'll immediately understand that you're about to have a not-so-ordinary wine-tasting experience.

Move from barrel to barrel sampling plenty of wine as you go. You'll even be able to request more of your favorites to top up, which is what probably earned this winery the nickname "Dumplotto."

As you will find out, many people have the same experience here. As you circulate around the cave, you'll find yourself laughing all the way. This wine tour is packed with anecdotes, jokes, and shared smiles, which become more evident as you move throughout the tour.

1445 St. Helena Hwy. South, St. Helena
707-963-2134

1055 Atlas Peak Rd., Napa
707-963-2134
www.deldottovineyards.com

TIP
The winery is open on Christmas and New Year's Day (but call to make sure). Do not get the wrong idea with all the fun they have. Del Dotto takes its wine seriously, with many awards for its wine and food pairings. Have fun!

TASTE NATURE
AT NAPA VALLEY OLIVE OIL MFG

As you head down Charter Oak passing Charter Oak restaurant on your left and Farmstead restaurant on your right, you won't expect what you're about to experience when you arrive at the end of the street at the Napa Valley Olive Oil MFG. This manufactory was established in 1931. Old-world charm is the best way to describe this place. They produce about twenty different balsamic vinegars and twenty different olive oils. Customer service is what stands out—the experience and knowledge of the products is quite evident when they help you.

Bring cash, as you'll need it. You can also grab more Italian items to take with you. Many delicacies that can only be imported from Italy are sold here. Stock up on your olive oil and have it shipped home. Be sure to take home the olive oil mixed with lemon. This is worth a quick stop when you're in St. Helena. I would love to see what you buy!

835 Charter Oak , St. Helena
707-963-4173
www.nvoliveoilmfg.com

FEEL LIKE PART OF THE FAMILY AND EXPERIENCE OLD NAPA VALLEY
AT THE HISTORIC REGUSCI WINERY

Wine Country doesn't get more authentic or breathtaking than this winery. Set against a dramatic backdrop in the Stags Leap Palisades, Regusci Winery is one of Napa Valley's most historic and memorable properties. Here you will experience a rustic glimpse of a Napa Valley that once was, as you explore sustainable gardens, a "ghost winery" from the 1800s, and renowned Bordeaux wines.

Since 1932 the Regusci family has carved a living from their scenic property in the Stags Leap District. From hay, walnuts, and plums to wine grapes, the Regusci name has been synonymous with world-class farming for five generations. Believers that wine is grown and not merely made, the Reguscis operate a family ranch that is home to one hundred and sixty pristine acres of Cabernet Sauvignon, Merlot, and Old Vine Zinfandel. This winery is one of a kind!

5584 Silverado Trail, Napa
707-254-0403
www.regusciwinery.com

TIP

Make a reservation so the winery knows you are coming, and join its club to ensure that you do not miss any new releases. Be sure to bring cash to purchase some fruit or vegetables from their "honor system" farmers market stand.

FEED YOUR SOUL
WITH SOME ARTISTIC FOOD
AT MORIMOTO

Sushi, tempura, nigiri, and sashimi are just a few dishes that make Japanese food great. Morimoto Napa is the Wine Country's leading Japanese restaurant, and it has definitely made its mark on the region's culinary scene.

This contemporary Japanese fusion restaurant specializes in bringing together the East and West. From artistic-looking sushi to locally grown fresh produce, Morimoto's plates are not only fresh but also aesthetically pleasing. Satisfy your appetite, and treat your taste buds to an explosion of exciting flavors and blends that will surely delight. What's it going to be? Rock shrimp tempura or hamachi tacos?

610 Main St., Napa
707-252-1600
www.morimotonapa.com

EXPLORE THE WORLD OF FILM
AT THE NAPA VALLEY FILM FESTIVAL

Poetry, beauty, horror, love . . . you'll witness all these and much more at this greatly anticipated annual cinematic event in Napa Valley.

Over a few chaotic days, the festival's main aim is to knock down any potential barriers between the artist and his or her audience. You'll be treated to never-before-screened independent films, some old classics, celebrity tributes, hot red-carpet parties, and much more.

As big foodies, we have to mention the food and wine as well as the outstanding cinematography. More than fifty esteemed chefs and one hundred fifty wineries take part in the festival, allowing you to sample even more gastronomical delights from the region.

1400 W Clay St. #100, Napa
707-226-7500
www.nvff.org

TIP
To ensure optimal reach, all competition films are screened a few times in different venues throughout the Valley, so if you miss one screening, check the program for the next one.

GRAB SOME OF THE BEST ITALIAN FOOD OUTSIDE OF ITALY
AT OTTIMO, YOUNTVILLE

They say that to get the best food in town you need to go where the locals go! If you're a little tired of dining out or having formal meals, head to this little Italian gem that the locals flock to. Okay, this might be premature because they just opened this year, and maybe not everyone has heard about it just yet. But they do know the creator Chef Michael Chiarello. From his world-class Bottega Restaurant (right next door) with the best "polenta under glass" antipasti to his brand-new Burger restaurant in the same village in Yountville, Chiarello knows food, and he knows how to execute it for everyone to enjoy.

"Ottimo" in Italian means optimal, first rate, excellent. This new eatery brings everything Italian together—pizza, fresh Mozzarella, coffee, wine, beer, and other handcrafted Italian products for you to enjoy in a casual setting. They serve lunch and breakfast every day, and they open at 8:00 a.m. The menu is simple, with pastries, breakfast pizzas, and fresh juices, along with mimosas and coffee from the espresso bar. You do not want to miss this place on your trip to Yountville.

Ottimo
6525 Washington St., Yountville
707-944-0102
www.ottimo-nv.com

Bottega
V Marketplace
6525 Washington St., Yountville
707-945-1050
www.botteganapavalley.com

GATHER WITH FRIENDS
ON THE GARDEN PATIO AT THE CALISTOGA INN RESTAURANT

Probably one of the most popular outdoor dining spots in the entire Valley, the Calistoga Inn Restaurant is the perfect place for locals and visitors to unwind al fresco.

With a long, minimalistic patio that seamlessly stretches along the bank of the Napa River together with the restaurant's very own award-winning microbrewery, you'll love everything about this Calistoga hot spot—from the craft ales right down to the easygoing atmosphere. The hotel is very reasonably priced, and European-style accommodations with shared bathrooms are available. You have to try their chicken wings. The sauce is historic!

1250 Lincoln Ave., Calistoga
707-942-4101
www.calistogainn.com

DISCOVER THE MAGIC
OF THE FRENCH LAUNDRY

For a truly magical dining experience, head to The French Laundry. More than just dinner, The French Laundry is a performance at every level.

It may test your patience getting a seat, but scheduling a stop at this restaurant is a must. Since it is one of the hottest restaurants in town, you'll have to do some forward thinking and book ahead!

Every day will be a surprise regarding the food, as the menu changes daily. Whatever is being served, however, you're in for a treat. Imagine feasting on Royal Kaluga caviar or herb-roasted Elysian Fields Farm lamb. Yum!

I always get asked is it worth it and I always say without hesitation "YES!"

6640 Washington St., Yountville
707-944-2380
www.thomaskeller.com

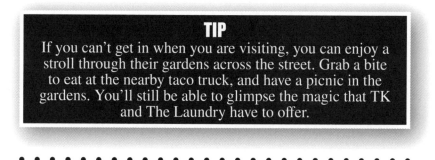

TIP
If you can't get in when you are visiting, you can enjoy a stroll through their gardens across the street. Grab a bite to eat at the nearby taco truck, and have a picnic in the gardens. You'll still be able to glimpse the magic that TK and The Laundry have to offer.

GRAB A FAMOUS COCKTAIL
AT ST. HELENA'S GOOSE & GANDER

Cocktails and a bite to eat in Walter Martini's old bungalow known as Goose & Gander, is the perfect way to end your day after a few "busy" hours of wine tasting.

Dine al fresco on the patio looking out into the garden, or request a seat indoors, where you'll see firsthand what the chefs do best. The Basement Bar is trendy, and the skilled mixologists offer a delicious and well-balanced cocktail that will suit your tastes. Walter's Manhattan is a must. You can't leave the Valley without having at least one!

G&G is a true gathering hub that celebrates authentic American dishes paired beautifully with drinks from its extensive list. One of the best experiences before you die is to attend their NYE bash. It might become your tradition each year. #FergusGG

1245 Spring St., St. Helena
707-967-8779
www.goosegander.com

TIP

Try the G&G burger with foie gras and bone marrow with duck fat fries.
Pair it with the Manhattan and you will have one of the best combinations your senses will ever experience. I'm not the only one who thinks so. It was also once recommended by "Napa Man" (www.napaman.com), and it's been a hit ever since!

DISCOVER EXCLUSIVENESS IN A BOTTLE
AT HARLAN ESTATE

Traveling up to Harlan Estate Winery, which has been aptly called the ultimate "cult winery," is worth it just for the views. You'll be treated to the "raw" and "wild" side of Napa Valley as you traverse the steep terraces that look out across the intriguing misty layers below.

Harlan Estate was established in Oakville's western hills in 1984. Spanning an impressive two hundred forty acres of pure beauty, the Estate benefits from both sedimentary and volcanic bedrock, which has allowed for its vertical terraced vineyards to produce top-quality Cabernet Sauvignon, Merlot, Cabernet Franc, and Petit Verdot wines.

Having created an exclusive name for itself within California and farther afield, Harlan Estate produces some of the most esteemed wines in the region, with an average price per bottle of $821.

707-944-1441
www.harlanestate.com

CATCH A MOVIE THE OLD-SCHOOL WAY
AT CAMEO CINEMA

This is classic cinema viewing at its finest. Cameo Cinema has a long history that dates back more than a hundred years, and this family-friendly community hub has become an integral part of entertainment in the region.

Sit back in the large, comfy seats and be entertained by film. It's a place where friends, family, and neighbors gather to daydream, ponder, laugh, and cry.

This old-school movie theater in St. Helena screens both recent releases and the golden oldies in a charming setting. You are able to enjoy a glass of wine or a beer in the comfort of your seat.

1340 Main St., St. Helena
707-963-0779
www.cameocinema.com

TIP
The Market, which is located across the street from Cameo Cinema, is the perfect post-show stop for some hearty American fare.

HEAD FOR A LITTLE LOCAL FLAVOR
AT COOK TAVERN

Like many other upvalley restaurants and bars in Napa Valley, the Cook Tavern, which can be reached by Highway 29, is a firm favorite among locals. With its host of beers and wines, it's no wonder that this small bar is a popular gathering spot.

The power duo of chefs holding the floor in this restaurant and the one next-door, cook quite spectacularly—a tavern filled with so much passion and talent. But whichever side you choose, you'll surely be impressed. The cuisine is visually and artistically pleasing to the eye as well as the palate. Relax and regroup at Cook restaurants, and recharge for your next adventure.

1304 Main St., St. Helena
707-963-8082

BECOME CULTURED
AT THE MUSIC IN THE VINEYARDS FESTIVAL

Music is a fundamental part of life in the Wine Country. Throughout the year, a number of events and festivals celebrate music. Given the location, it's often intertwined with the art of winemaking, and one of the most greatly anticipated events of the year is Music in the Vineyards.

Held without fail for three weeks every August, this music festival is nationally renowned, and people flock from near and far to enjoy listening to world-famous musicians perform.

A vineyard setting can evoke deep emotions. Add a classic chamber music repertoire to the mix, and it's something you've never experienced before.

1020 Clinton St., Napa
707-258-5559
www.musicinthevineyards.org

CELEBRATE FOOD, WINE,
AND CULTURE AT BRASSWOOD ESTATE

Probably one of the hottest new wineries in the area, the upvalley Brasswood Estate was born from the notion of wanting to share the story of Napa Valley through contemplative visual and tasting experiences. One of the leading wineries, Brasswood is also home to some of the most sought-after winemakers on the winery estate. You will find such winemakers as Philipe Melka, Angelina Mondavi, Russell Bevans, Rosemary Cakebread, Tim Milos, Stacia Dowdell, and Jason Moore, just to name a few. Some of their wines are sold out, but you can go to Brasswood's website to find out where their wines are available to taste or purchase.

For a unique sensory Brasswood experience, stop in to the visual olfactory room maintained by the property sommelier.

Explore this inimitable winery that offers tailor-made tours, intimate tastings, unique dining experiences, and much more.

With a chic restaurant on-site, you can try a range of tantalizing dishes that epitomize the comfort and culture of Napa Valley. The pulled Mozzerella is a must, just ask anyone who's dined here before. When it is heirloom tomato season, this pairing is . . . perfect!

3111 St. Helena Hwy., St. Helena,
707-968-5434
www.brasswood.com

TIP

Brasswood's winemaker Stacia Dowdell and consulting winemaker Angelina Mondavi make some of the best Cabernet Sauvignon from their estate vineyard in the Coombsville appellation. You can spend a whole day at Brasswood!

GET READY TO INDULGE
AT THE CHARTER OAK

The greatest oak was once a nut that held its ground . . . You will find this quote in the restaurant that says it best. The Charter Oak is the newest restaurant that has hit the scene in 2017 not only in St. Helena but also in Napa Valley. The detail shown in the ingredients of the menu and in the restaurant itself makes you feel the vision right away. Owners Christopher Kostow and Nathaniel Dorn of the Michelin three-starred restaurant at Meadowood have given us a place to enjoy without having to commit to a three-star experience. The seasonal food reflects the products of Napa Valley with an elemental cooking style, centered on the hearth, highlighting one or two ingredients at a time. The bar shares the same passion. Stay close to town in one of St. Helena's great hotels and walk home when you're done. One of my favorite boutique hotels is the Wydown Hotel (www.wydownhotel.com). The cocktails are balanced and classic—my new favorite is the Flip. Do not miss their Sunday brunch. Their posole soup is the best I have ever had.

1050 Charter Oak Ave., St. Helena
707-302-6996
www.thecharteroak.com

TIP

If you can't get a reservation, go to the bar and sit out on the patio, where you can either stare at the wood-burning kitchen area or through the bar into the dining room and see all the action. These two tables will add to the entertainment experience. They serve a limited menu in the bar that will fill your cravings but leave you wanting to try more.

GO SPANISH AND EAT TAPAS
AT NAPA'S ZUZU

Perfectly placed on Napa's picturesque riverfront in the Downtown area, you'll find Zuzu, a cozy Spanish restaurant serving up a range of what can only be described as well-executed tapas paired with outstanding wines, which include a number of well-known Spanish varietals together with local favorites.

Unpretentious with a relaxed and casual atmosphere, Zuzu imparts a buzz in the constantly bustling dining room that will immediately feel like home away from home.

829 Main St., Napa
707-224-8555
www.zuzunapa.com

TIP

In a true tapas-style restaurant, there are no reservations, so it can get busy, but don't be dismayed. If you can't get a table immediately, your delectable tapas dishes can also be served at the bar while you wait!

LEARN ABOUT SUSTAINABLE FARMING AND WINE
AT FROG'S LEAP WINERY

For an unpretentious wine experience, Frog's Leap Winery is just the place. If ever there were to be an "iconic" California winery, this would be it.

Housed in a stunning Victorian property and located in Rutherford, this winery, which is dedicated to producing world-class wines from organically grown grapes, offers a relaxed approach for enjoying wine.

Known for their easy hospitality, the staff at Frog's Leap will instantly make you feel welcome. You'll find the humor refreshing, which is evident by their motto: "Time's fun when you're having flies."

The winery's award-winning Cabernet Sauvignon and Chardonnay have earned this Rutherford appellation winery it's "forever" spot on the Napa Valley winemaking map.

8815 Conn Creek Rd., Rutherford
707-963-4704
www.frogsleap.com

TIP

Designated drivers don't have to miss out at Frog's Leap Winery. Ask for the unique "water tasting," which consists of four fruit-infused waters.

DISCOVER CAVE CELLARS
ON HOWELL MOUNTAIN

When you enter the area, you won't be able to recognize immediately that Howell Mountain is responsible for producing some of the best Cabernet Sauvignon in Napa Valley. Instead of following roads with rolling vineyards, you'll travel through a thicket of trees that will eventually lead you to a number of modest estates.

Howell Mountain's wine production history is curious. Back in the 1870s, two fortunate men planted vines on cheap mountain land to cut costs, which clearly proved to be a blessing, as today it's one of the more renowned Cabernet Sauvignon regions in the world.

Black Sears Estate Wines
2610 Summit Lake Dr., Angwin
707-889-1243, www.blacksears.com

Robert Foley Vineyards
1300 Summit Lake Dr., Angwin
707-965-2669, www.robertfoleyvineyards.com

Retro Cellars
1955 Summit Lake Dr., Angwin
707-965-1042, www.retrocellars.com

Neal Family Vineyards
716 Liparita Ave., Angwin
707-965-2800, www.nealvineyards.com

TIP

Howell Mountain is home to some of the best cave tours you'll find off the beaten track in the Valley. These are Napa's secret spots. Some awesome underground caves worth exploring include Robert Foley, Retro Cellars, and Neal Family Vineyards.

WALK UNDER A PARASOL
AT CROCKER & STARR WINERY

Crocker & Starr Winery has been producing top-quality wines that exude both power and balance for a number of years. Located just off California Highway 29, you'll be pleasantly surprised at your discovery.

With a tasteful mix of modern and traditional, this historic farmhouse and winery overlook a sprawling, meticulously maintained vineyard that spans some eighty-five acres.

Upon arrival, you'll be warmly greeted with a glass of wine by a welcoming tasting host who'll ease you into the tasting experience. Attention to detail is evident from the inviting porch to a wicker basket containing a number of colorful parasols for guests.

700 Dowdell Lane, St. Helena
707-967-9111
www.crockerstarr.com

TIP
Buy their Cabernet Franc and Sauvignon Blanc—some of the best wine made in Napa Valley.

CATCH A FEW RAYS AND SIP SOME BUBBLY
AT MUMM NAPA WINERY

Nicknamed "a complex sparkler," Mumm Napa sparkling wine features on many a table for special occasions. Join a memorable tour of a winery that's responsible for producing one of the most wedding-worthy wines around. We guarantee that you'll walk away with at least a few bottles. You don't even need a celebratory excuse!

While the entire tour of Mumm Napa is fabulous, the highlight has to be the outdoor wine tasting among the vines. Spring and summer visitors should book the Oak Terrace Tasting, which allows you to catch a few rays while sipping on your award-winning bubbly.

8445 Silverado Trail, Napa
707-967-7700
www.mummnapa.com

TIP
Take a stroll through Mumm Napa's fine art photography gallery with a glass of wine in hand, and lose yourself in a world of photographic artwork.

SHOPPING AND FASHION

SHINE BRIGHT
LIKE A DIAMOND

Shrouded in tasteful classic jewelry cases with displays fit for royalty, Patina Estate and Palladium Fine Jewelry in the heart of St. Helena offer some of the finest and most exclusive pieces in the region.

When you walk into these two stores owned by two amazing jewelers, you will lose track of time. Patina is a vintage house, filled with history and classic pieces that tell stories of the era they came from. Palladium is a magical and enchanting jewelry house, whether you are selecting a piece for a lifetime commitment or a spontaneous statement piece for the evening. These shops hold court directly across the street from each other, and you will find yourself going back and forth until you decide which stunning piece fits your mood—new or old. This will be a one-of-a-kind experience, and you will find yourself planning your next trip to Napa Valley around wanting to find new pieces to add to your collection. This is one I would love to see. #100ThingsNapaValley.

Patina Estate & Fine Jewelry
1342 Main St., St. Helena
707-963-5445

Palladium Fine Jewelry
1339 Main St., St. Helena
707-963-5900

DON'T ROAM TOO FAR

The charming antique shops and vintage boutiques in the Valley are always buzzing. Even if you're not looking for anything in particular, it's always fun to browse. You just never know what you're going to find. Roam is exactly what this place does. They Roam the world in search of the most interesting antiques to offer their clients and customers. Roam specializes in winemaking artifacts.

You will find tools and old equipment used in California and as far away as Europe. They have a great eye for style because they are the same family that brought Napa Valley Mario's Men's Store more than thirty years ago. Roam is located on Calistoga's main street.

If you're looking for vintage wine-related objects, this is your place. They are always about finding the right piece for their clients, and they encourage you to email them if you are interested in selling a whole estate or specific antiques.

1124 Lincoln Ave., Calistoga
707-942-4508
www.roamantiques.com

SHOP TILL YOUR HEART'S CONTENT
ON ST. HELENA'S MAIN STREET

Ask anyone. The shopping in St. Helena is some of the best anywhere! Even if you're not a shopaholic, you'll be enamored by the sheer selection. My favorite store is Mario's. I've been buying clothes there since the late '90s. The sheer quality of clothes it selects, plus the service, is like having your own personal shopper in your home closet. You wear a lot of jeans in Napa Valley, and they have them for any occasion. If you're old enough to remember the gentleman's shoe and clothing stores of the past, this place feels like that. Shoehorns, cufflinks, sports coats, and jackets are just a few items they have for sale. You can find almost anything you need for any Napa Valley occasion or dinner party. If you are coming to Napa Valley for a wedding, this is a place where you can rent a tuxedo. There is no need to travel with one. Just rent it before you come and leave it before you leave. Mario's seems to always be on the leading edge of male fashion. Stop in and let them know Marcus sent you!

1223 Main St., St. Helena
707-963-1603

TIP

After you max out your credit card shopping at Mario's, right next door are the best sandwiches in Napa Valley at Giugni's Deli. They only accept cash, but after shopping you will enjoy using cash.

SAMPLE EXQUISITE WINES
IN JCB'S LUXURIOUS SURREALIST ROOM

For wine tasting in Napa Valley, nothing is more exquisite and luxurious than experiencing the JCB Tasting Salon in Yountville. This one-of-a-kind wine-tasting room perfectly combines a collection of fine wines and luxury products.

Created by Jean-Charles Boisset, this unique wine-tasting destination seamlessly encompasses fashion and a luxury lifestyle. Take the opportunity to admire (and purchase if you wish) some of JCB's custom-designed jewelry while sampling some high-quality wines.

Step into the intimate Surrealist Room with a JCB wine expert for a flight you'll never forget. A number of tasting packages are available, so choose the one that best suits your style.

6505 Washington St., Yountville
707-967-7600
www.jcbcollection.com

Raymond Vineyards
849 Zinfandel Ln., St. Helena
707-963-3141
www.raymondvineyards.com

TIP
Raymond Vineyard is JCB's sister winery. You can continue the celebration and discover this beautiful property.

EQUIP YOURSELF WITH THE PERFECT BIKE
FROM ST. HELENA CYCLERY

When in doubt, pedal it out.

With a long history and an unsurpassable reputation in the Valley, St. Helena Cyclery has been serving cycling enthusiasts since 1979.

Choose the bike to suit your level, from Trek Carbon Domane road bikes to hybrids. With rental bikes and bikes for sale, this is one cycle shop that caters to everyone.

If this isn't enough, the knowledgeable team is ready to advise you on the bike to suit your body, fitness level, and needs. They'll also fill you in about all those hidden Napa biking trails that locals rave about!

1156 Main St., St. Helena
707-963-7736
www.sthelenacyclery.com

TIP
Can't go to the store and pick up your bike? No worries! St. Helena Cyclery will deliver right to your door!

MAKE YOUR DAY BETTER
WITH FRESHLY BAKED TREATS FROM THE MODEL BAKERY

You'll smell it before you reach it. The Model Bakery, as its name suggests, is the ideal bakery for all your baked needs and naughty vices. It's the one-stop shop for artisan breads, cakes, muffins, pastries, sandwiches, and much more. If it was good enough for Oprah, it's good for anyone. This place is where I meet more celebrities than anywhere else in Napa Valley.

The Model Bakery is one of the oldest of its kind in California. Yes, you read correctly . . . not just Napa Valley but the entire state! Having been in operation for more than ninety years, this establishment has had a great deal of time to perfect its specialities, which range from salted caramel chocolate chip gourmet cookies to well-risen fresh English muffins (Oprah's favorites).

1357 Main St., St. Helena
707-963-8192, www.themodelbakery.com

644 1st St., Bldg. B, Napa
707-259-1128, www.themodelbakery.com

6523 Washington St. Yountville
www.themodelbakery.com

TIP

If you need something quick, grab one of the bakery's delicious prewrapped sandwiches to have on the go.

GET YOUR CHOCOLATE FIX
AT THE BEST CHOCOLATE HOUSE IN AMERICA

Cabernet and chocolate . . . mmm, they're a match made in heaven! We're not sure if the Wine Country's great chocolate establishments are coincidental or people knew a number of certified chocoholics were living here, but either way, on top of our world-class wines and first-rated cuisine, the Valley is home to some amazing chocolate stores.

According to the *Huffington Post*, Woodhouse Chocolate was named the best chocolate shop in America. I would say it also has the best window displays in America. Walking by their store almost every day I am always in awe of their chocolate displays. If it's not a giant Easter Bunny during the spring or gardening tools made of chocolate during the fall, it is something equally impressive and worth a picture. Once you are done staring, go inside and buy enough chocolate to fulfill your craving. Their attention to detail only supports the amazing ingredients they use to make these edible jewels.

Woodhouse Chocolate
1367 Main St., St. Helena
800-966-3468

Anette's
1321 1st St., Napa
707-252-4228
www.anettes.com

Vintage Sweet Shop
530 St. B, Napa
707-224-2986
www.vintagesweetshoppe.com

Kollar Chocolates
6525 Washington St., Yountville
707-738-6750
www.kollarchocolates.com

DISCOVER
NAPA'S BUSTLING FARMERS MARKETS

Who doesn't love a good farmers market? If you're in Napa Valley, there's no better place to experience what it's really like to live in the Wine Country.

Napa's farmers markets are more than just fresh food. They also offer many other interesting items, such as handmade gifts, jewelry, homemade fragrances, and clothing. Mellow live music often plays softly in the background to set the scene, and the smell of aromatic fresh coffee lingers in the air. Also be sure to sample the freshly baked pastries!

Napa Farmers Market
South Napa Century Center, 195 Gassed Dr., Napa
707-501-3087, www.napafarmersmarket.org

Oxbow Public Market
610 & 644 1st St., Napa
707-226-6529, www.oxbowpublicmarket.com

St. Helena Farmers Market
Crane Park, 360 Crane Ave., St. Helena
707-486-2662, www.sthelenafarmersmkt.org

Long Meadow Ranch Farmers Market
738 Main St., St. Helena
707-963-4555, www.longmeadowranch.com

SUGGESTED ITINERARIES

NOT JUST FOR HONEYMOONERS

Go on a Hot Air Balloon Adventure aloft the Valley, 38

Catch a Few Rays and Sip Some Bubbly at Mumm
Napa Winery, 125

See Where East Meets West at Newton Vineyards, 58

Stop off at PRESS and Savor its Blends, 79

Have a Romantic Stay at Auberge du Soleil, 66

EXPERIENCE NAPA VALLEY WITH NO REGRETS

Discover Exclusiveness in a Bottle of Harlan Estate, 110

Immerse Yourself in Splendor at Schramsberg Vineyard, 92

Discover the Magic of French Laundry, 107

Enjoy a Luxury Stay at Meadowood, 84

• •

WINE AND NOTHING ELSE

EAT YOUR HEART OUT!

INDEX

● ●